Never Settle For Good Enough
Workbook

A Simplified Guide to a Better Marriage

Kendall and Starla Bridges

Copyright © 2019 Kendall and Starla Bridges
All rights reserved.

ISBN: 978-1-7331227-1-9

Contents

Guidelines for Getting the Most Out of This Workbook...........................7

Commitment Agreement 9

Chapter One:...13

Chapter Two:...33

    Personality Strengths and Weaknesses Chart 43

Chapter Three:...51

Chapter Four:..67

Chapter Five:..81

Bonus Chapter – SEX!...95

Closing Statement...103

Resources and Recommendations 104

Here We Go . . .

Welcome to the *Never Settle For Good Enough Workbook*. This is a place where you begin the process of a better-than-average marriage. This is where the rubber meets the road, where ideas become reality, where theory is put into practice, where plans and convictions become actions, where we go from talking the talk to walking the walk. This is where we make a life change by committing to our spouse that we will never stop pursuing God, pursuing them and pursuing a beautiful marriage for the rest of our lives.

Are you ready? LET'S DO THIS!

We are so excited for what God has in store for your marriage!

—Kendall and Starla Bridges

Guidelines for Getting the Most
Out of This Workbook

1. Don't rush through it.

2. Don't get overwhelmed.

3. Read one chapter of the book *Never Settle For Good Enough* together. Then sit down and talk through the same chapter and discussion questions in this Workbook—either together or separately. Then, share your answers with each other—preferably, one chapter per week. (Maybe just before you go on your weekly date night!) Then, repeat each week.

4. Answer truthfully.

5. Go into this selflessly, not selfishly. Your attitude should not be, "What will this do for my spouse?" but "What will this do for me?"

6. Go into this unoffended. Don't allow your spouse's answers to offend you. Talk through each answer. Find the common ground.

7. Be committed to improve.

8. Be committed to change.

9. Be committed to do whatever it takes to have a Better Marriage.

10. Be committed to the process and follow through.

"Never settle for good enough. It can always be better."

Commitment Agreement

1. I Will Never Settle For Good Enough.
   It Can Always Be Better.

2. I will not allow this process to be a source of contention.

3. I will make sure that we always take the high road and remain positive and respectful.

4. I will be open and honest, as well as kind and considerate.

5. I will not use what you share with me as a way to get back at you.

_____   _____

Your signature   Your One and Only

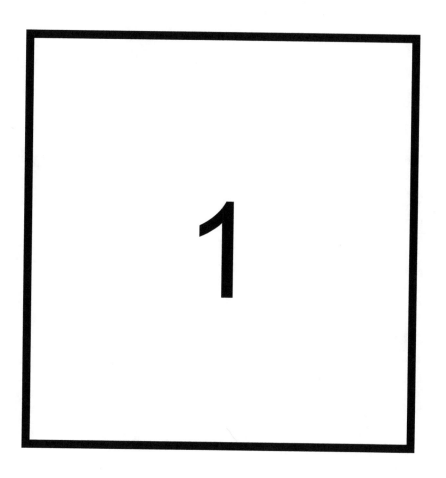

Chapter One

―――――――――――――――――――――――――――

But seek first his kingdom and his righteousness, and all these things will be given to you as well.

—Matthew 6:33

"The key is not to prioritize what's on your schedule, but to schedule your priorities."

—Stephen Covey

QUESTION AND ANSWER EXERCISE

Answer these questions:

1. What do you love most about your spouse?

_____
_____
_____
_____
_____
_____

2. What was the first thing that attracted you to your spouse?

_____
_____
_____
_____
_____

3. When dating, what was the one thing they said or did that made you think, "I want to marry him/her!"?

_____

_____

_____

_____

_____

Choose to focus more on your answers above because the very things that brought you together could be the very things that keeps you together.

List your Top 5 priorities:

1.

2.

3.

4.

5.

Now compare your list with your spouse's to see how closely your priorities align.

The Bible teaches us that God made the husband and wife to be one flesh, one team, and partners in a shared vision.

> *Then the LORD God made a woman from the rib he had taken out of the man, and he brought her to the man. The man said, "This is now bone of my bones and flesh of my flesh; she shall be called 'woman,' for she was taken out of man."*
>
> *—Genesis 2:22-23*

First Priority: God

"You shall have no other gods before me."

—Exodus 20:3

This is the first of the 10 commandments. It simply means God should be the first priority in our lives. It is impossible to live your best life without God being first.
How do we live out putting God first in our lives?

A. Prayer

This is the confidence we have in approaching God: that if we ask anything according to his will, he hears us. And if we know that he hears us—whatever we ask—we know that we have what we asked of him.

—1 John 5:14-15 (NIV)

Here is a simple plan for prayer each day—A.C.T.S.:

A—Adoration. Take a few minutes and just worship and adore Jesus Christ. Put on your favorite worship song and do nothing but worship.

C—Confession. 1 John 1:9 says, *"If we confess our sins, he is faithful and just to forgives of our sins and to cleanse from all unrighteousness."* Take this time to confess any known or unknown sins.

T—Thanksgiving. Take a moment and just thank God for all He has done. Thank Him for the three things you are most thankful for today.

S—Supplication. This means to simply ask Him for what you need today. God cares and He hears. Just ask.

B. Bible Reading

All Scripture is God-breathed and is useful for teaching, rebuking, correcting and training in righteousness, so that the servant of God may be thoroughly equipped for every good work.

—2 Timothy 3:16-17 (NIV)

Download a Bible reading plan at youversion.com or a daily devotional at kendallbridges.com

C. Church Attendance

And let us consider how we may spur one another on toward love and good deeds, not giving up meeting together, as some are in the habit of doing, but encouraging one another—and all the more as you see the Day approaching.

—**Hebrews 10:24-25 (NIV)**

Second Priority: Marriage

God is first. Marriage is second. Period. If you love God first, you'll love each other better.

Husbands, love your wives, just as Christ loved the church and gave himself up for her.

—**Ephesians 5:25**

"Then they can urge the younger women to love their husbands and children."

—**Titus 2:4**

A. What does that look like?

Weekly—Date night (no children*). Alternate who gets to choose what this date looks like. That way, you don't end up at the same burger joint with 14 sports TV screens each week. (Sorry guys, trying to help you not screw this up!)

* Childcare: Don't use the excuse that you don't have a sitter to watch your kids. Find someone you trust (who is likeminded) and your kids enjoy being with. If you can't afford a sitter, find a couple you can trade off with. Time together with your spouse is so important to the health of your marriage.

Monthly—Overnight stay away from the house (no children).

Quarterly—Weekend away from the house (children optional).

Yearly—One-week vacation with kids.

There are so many ways to make this happen, even on a shoestring budget.

Losers make excuses, winners find a way.

B. Having stated priorities and an agreed upon purpose as a couple is a must for a successful family.

Third Priority—Children

He and all his family were devout and God-fearing;

—Acts 10:2 (NIV)

A. Husbands and wives have to be committed to God first, one another second and then your children third. Why?

1. God is first because we will spend all of eternity with Him.

2. Spouse is second because this is until death do us part.

3. Children are third because they are a temporary assignment. You have them through their childhood. Hopefully, you will raise them to serve God and to understand God's plan for marriage, and they will start families of their own.

We understand that God is first, my marriage is second and my children are third. How do we create a healthy environment for our family?

B. Three ways to create a healthy environment for your family: Be There, Be Aware, and Be Fair.

- _____—Just be present. Physically and mentally.

  Pray together. Play together. Stay together. Read the Bible together. Read a family devotional book together. Find what works best for your family. Having devotions at breakfast worked best for our children.

- _____—Pay attention to what they are saying (your spouse and your children). Pay attention to what they want to do and where they want to go. Our kids will talk—if they know we will listen.

- _____—Spend enough quality time with your spouse and each of your children (boys and girls).

You are the number one example to your kids on how to "do life." They are watching you and mimicking you. They will come to you first to ask "life" questions. Don't brush them off; don't push them away—if you do, they'll go elsewhere to learn. This molding time with your children is precious and it will be gone before you know it.

Do your best, God will do the rest, and He will give you children who will serve the Lord.

Fourth Priority: Church

Every family needs a church family to be a part of and to grow in. A great church will help in the development of both of you as a husband and as a wife, and will also help disciple your children in the Word of God.

And let us consider how we may spur one another on toward love and good deeds, not giving up meeting together, as some are in the habit of doing, but encouraging one another—and all the more as you see the Day approaching.

—Hebrews 10:24-25 (NIV)

"Planted in the house of the LORD, they will flourish in the courts of our God. They will still bear fruit in old age, they will stay fresh and green..."

—Psalm 92:13-14

We know from experience that sports, music lessons, vacations, and family nights are all wonderful, fun and necessary in the lives of your kids and family. BUT don't ever let any of these things come before God—spending time with Him alone, together as a couple and worshipping as a family. Teach your children how to prioritize their lives at a young age. Their relationship with God should never be in the shadow of sports, hobbies, fun, friends—not even academics.

You need to figure out what works best for your family. Every family is different, but these are three areas (Prayer, Bible Reading and Church Attendance) that are non-negotiable. You must make them a priority in your daily and weekly life.

Fifth Priority: Extended Family and Friends

A. Extended Family

There is a reason why God says in **Genesis 2:24** (KJV), *Therefore shall a man **leave** his father and his mother, and shall **cleave** unto his wife: and they shall be one flesh.*

1. When you get married, it's time to grow up and leave your parents. When we walked down the aisle together as husband and wife, we were making a statement that we have left our parents and are now joined together as "one."

2. This doesn't mean that we cut all ties, but you do need to establish your own family, your own rules and your own traditions.

B. Friends

1. We all need friends, but we do not need to allow our friends to become more

important than our relationship with God, our family, and our ability to provide for our family.

Walk with the wise and become wise, for a companion of fools suffers harm.

—**Proverbs 13:20**

A friend loves at all times, and a brother is born for a time of adversity.

—**Proverbs 17:17**

As iron sharpens iron, so one person sharpens another.

—**Proverbs 27:17**

2. Whenever we allow things in our life to get out of priority, we are risking throwing away the very things that are most valuable to us.

When we allow work, friends, or other relationships to be more important than our marriage or when we allow distractions in our marriage, we run the risk of destroying the most beautiful relationship that God has given to mankind: the marriage.

There is no one who knows you more intimately and cares for you more deeply, and there is no one who understands you or believes in you more than your one and only.

Sixth Priority: Work

Anyone who does not provide for their relatives, and especially for their own household, has denied the faith and is worse than an unbeliever.

—**1 Timothy 5:8 (NIV)**

For even when we were with you, we gave you this rule: "The one who is unwilling to work shall not eat."

—**2 Thessalonians 3:10 (NIV)**

A. Every family is different in the matter of a vocation. Obviously, there has been a major shift in women in the workplace. Not as many stay at home as before. I don't think there is a simple, right or wrong answer. But there is a right or wrong for your family. Each couple has to agree on what works best for their home. This is a discussion that needs to happen before marriage, if at all possible.

B. A successful marriage is about working through the potential landmines that tend to blow up marriages. You need to come to a place of agreement. You must find the win-win for both husband and wife. That is the result of successfully navigating through a disagreement. Not just one person wins, but both find a way to win through compromise.

Seventh Priority: Hobbies and Interests

A. Having a hobby or an interest is good and healthy. But everything has to be in balance. It is important that you negotiate a balance that is a win-win for each of you. This is not the time to hold your ground. This is the perfect opportunity to give a little or even a lot on each side, in order to find the right balance for your marriage.

B. Your defined purposed and priorities could be the very thing that saves your marriage. Better marriages have something to look forward to together.

Simplified

Remember, whatever your priorities are, whether good or bad, they become the magnetic draw for your focus and, eventually, your destiny. This will be the guiding force for your life. You will continue to move in the direction of your priorities.

When priorities are in the proper place, anything is possible. But when our priorities are out of place, it's hard to accomplish anything.

Proper Priorities

1. God

2. Marriage

3. Children

4. Church

5. Work

6. Extended Family and Friends

7. Hobbies and Interests

When we allow work, friends, or other relationships to be more important than our marriage, we run the risk of destroying the most beautiful relationship that God has given to mankind, the marriage.

Challenge: Together with your spouse, state your priorities and agree on what is most important in your marriage and family. Then, determine and agree on how you will guard your priorities and live them out each day.

Answer these two questions with each other. Imagine you are 100 years old. What do you wish you had spent more time on? What do you wish you had spent less time on?

_____

_____

_____

_____

Pray this today: *Lord, we commit today to put you first in all we do. We choose to seek first the Kingdom of God. We ask for your help, wisdom and grace to prioritize our marriage, family, work and friends in a way that honors you. Help us die to our selfish desires and keep your desires as our greatest goal.* **In Jesus' name, Amen.**

Discussion Questions

Rate yourself on a scale of 1-5, on whether or not your priorities are in proper order. (1 is poor, 5 is excellent) Share it.

1................................2................................3................................4................................5

1. Do you have stated priorities and unified purpose/shared dreams for your marriage? Share your dreams and goals with your spouse. Develop a dream together.

_____
_____
_____
_____
_____
_____
_____
_____

2. Do you put God first in your marriage? If so, how?

_____
_____
_____
_____
_____
_____
_____
_____

3. What do you struggle with more: Prayer, Bible Reading or Church Attendance? Why?

_____
_____
_____
_____
_____
_____
_____

4. Do you put your spouse first—before the children? If so, how?

_____
_____
_____
_____
_____
_____
_____

5. In what ways have you put your children before your marriage relationship?

_____
_____
_____
_____
_____
_____
_____

6. How can you show your children that they matter to you?

_____
_____
_____
_____
_____
_____
_____

7. How do you manage work, family, church and friends?

_____
_____
_____
_____
_____
_____
_____

8. How have friends helped you through difficult times?

_____

_____

_____

_____

_____

_____

_____

9. How have friends interfered with your marriage?

_____

_____

_____

_____

_____

_____

_____

10. Are you in agreement regarding your extended family's role in your marriage? Explain.

_____

_____

_____

_____

_____

_____

_____

11. Are you in agreement regarding your friends' roles in your marriage? Explain.

_____

_____

_____

_____

_____

_____

_____

12. Are you in agreement regarding your hobbies and interests? Explain.

_____
_____
_____
_____
_____
_____
_____
_____

13. What steps can you take to make sure your priorities are in order?

_____
_____
_____
_____
_____
_____
_____

Use the notes section to write notes, thoughts, ideas or questions.

Notes:_____

_____

_____

_____

_____

_____

_____

_____

_____

_____

_____

_____

_____

_____

_____

_____

_____

_____

_____

_____

_____

_____

Use the notes section to write notes, thoughts, ideas or questions.

Notes:_____

_____

_____

_____

_____

_____

_____

_____

_____

_____

_____

_____

_____

_____

_____

_____

_____

_____

_____

Use the notes section to write notes, thoughts, ideas or questions.

Notes:_____

_____

_____

_____

_____

_____

_____

_____

_____

_____

_____

_____

_____

_____

_____

_____

_____

_____

_____

_____

Use the notes section to write notes, thoughts, ideas or questions.

Notes:_____

_____

_____

_____

_____

_____

_____

_____

_____

_____

_____

_____

_____

_____

_____

_____

_____

_____

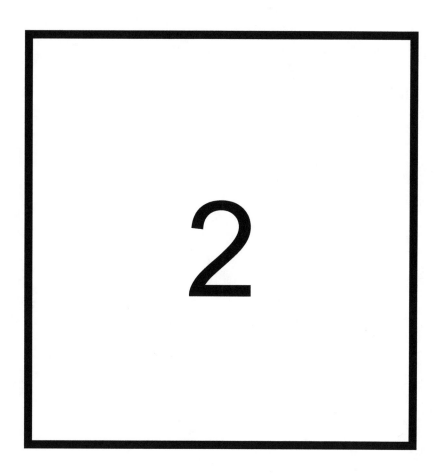

Chapter Two

Do not let any unwholesome talk come out of your mouths, but only what is helpful for building others up according to their needs, that it may benefit those who listen.

—Ephesians 4:29

"Wise men speak because they have something to say; Fools because they have to say something."

—Plato

Communication = (from the Latin commūnicāre meaning "to share") is the act of conveying intended meanings from one entity or group to another through the use of mutually understood signs and semiotic rules.

We would love to say that we have learned the art of communication and we totally get each other, but we would be lying. What we have learned is the beauty and value in communicating the right way.

Do we always agree on everything now? No, and we never will. Neither will you and your spouse, but that's okay; it's normal. Healthy marriages can still have conflict – you just need to learn how to handle it the right way.

PERSONALITIES

We found out really quickly, that we were complete opposites. But instead of accepting each other, we tried to change each other. We didn't recognize that our opposite personalities were actually a perfect match for a complete team. Crazy, huh? Who would have thought?

We want to encourage you and your spouse to take a personality test so that you can understand who you are and who your spouse is. This will be vital in learning to communicate and understand each other.

This is not a competition; there's not a "winner." Each trait has incredible gifts that are valuable to your success in every area of life. There are also negative aspects in each trait that can destroy your destiny.

Seriously, do it now...go to the website. Go to temperamentquiz.com for a free quick test to discover your personality.

Did you do it? Don't lie!

This teaching breaks the personality/temperament into four types: Sanguine, Melancholy, Choleric and Phlegmatic.

The ancient Greeks developed the first personality theory, which is where these terms come from. Your personality is formed primarily by both nature and nurture. Nature is the temperament you are born with and nurture is all the factors, including culture, family of origin, education, etc., that might help shape your personality.

- CHOLERIC –   The Doer, The Natural Leader, Determined, Energetic, Goal-Oriented.

- MELANCHOLY – The Thinker, The Perfectionist, Sensitive, Thoughtful, Quiet.

- PHLEGMATIC – The Watcher, The Peacemaker, Easy-Going, Calm, Chill.

- SANGUINE – The Talker, The Life of the Party, Enthusiastic, Fun-Loving, Outgoing.

Each of you will most likely be a combination of two traits. There is a complete chart with a description of each temperament on page 43 of this workbook.

COMMUNICATION 101

"Just say a simple, 'Yes, I will,' or 'No, I won't.' Your word is enough. If you have to strengthen your promise with a vow then something is wrong."

—Matthew 5:37 (NLT Paraphrased)

Those who love to talk will experience the consequences, for the tongue can kill or nourish life.

—Proverbs 18:21 (NLT)

Here are a few rules we all need to set in place before trying to communicate.

THE 9 T's OF COMMUNICATION

1.   *Time*   —Make time each and every day to really talk to each other.

   You do not know what tomorrow holds.

—James 4:14

2.   *Timing*   —Be considerate when it comes to the timing of more serious conversations.

   There is a time for everything

—Ecclesiastes 3:1

3.   *Tone*   —Be careful with the tone you use when talking with your spouse.

34

A gentle answer turns away wrath, but harsh words stir up anger.

—**Proverbs 15:1** (NLT)

4. _____—Listen, really listen and hear your spouse when they are speaking.

My dear brothers and sisters, be quick to listen, slow to speak, and slow to get angry.

—**James 1:19** (NLT)

5. _____—Be certain that the words you speak to your spouse are like treasure … good, helpful and encouraging!

Don't use foul or abusive language. Let everything you say be good and helpful, so that your words will be an encouragement to those who hear them.

—**Ephesians 4:29** (NLT)

6. _____—Communicate as a team.

"Can two people walk together in unity without agreeing on a direction?"

—**Amos 3:3**

"Where there is unity there is always victory."

—**Publilius Syrus**

7. _____—When there is a conflict, if necessary, take a time-out, calm down and gather your composure before you continue to communicate.

"A hot-tempered person stirs up conflict, but the one who is patient calms a quarrel."

—*Proverbs 15:18*

8. _____—You cannot have a healthy marriage if you cannot be truthful.
"An honest answer is like a kiss on the lips."

—**Proverbs 24:26**

9. _____—Always be transparent with your spouse. No one loves you more or believes in you more than your one and only.

"We have spoken freely to you…our heart is wide open."

—**2 Corinthians 6:11**

"A wise man learns from the mistakes of others, a foolish man must learn from his own mistakes."

—**King Solomon (Paraphrased)**

Evaluate Yourself on Communication

(Rate yourself on a scale of 1-5, on each of the T's of communication. (1 is poor, 5 is excellent) Circle the number that best describes where you are.

TIME

1.........................2.........................3.........................4.........................5

TIMING

1.........................2.........................3.........................4.........................5

TONE

1.........................2.........................3.........................4.........................5

TUNE

1.........................2.........................3.........................4.........................5

TREASURE

1.........................2.........................3.........................4.........................5

TEAM

1.........................2.........................3.........................4.........................5

TIME-OUT

1.........................2.........................3.........................4.........................5

TRUTH

1.........................2.........................3.........................4.........................5

TRANSPARENCY

1.........................2.........................3.........................4.........................5

Disagreements

"Anyone, who loves to quarrel loves sin; anyone who speaks boastfully invites disaster."

—**Proverbs 17:19 (ESV Paraphrased)**

"Only fools get into constant quarrels."

—**Proverbs 18:6 (ESV Paraphrased)**

Make sure to refer to page 124 in our book *Better Marriage Against All Odds* for 10 Rules to Fight Fair.

Most Common Struggles In Marriage

*Communication
*Time (Not spending enough time together)
*Sex
*Work. (Too much time away/Not getting a job)
*Money
*Parenting
*Outside family interfering in our life
*A controlling spouse
*Technology addictions
*Lack of privacy, sharing too much with friends and on social media
*Secrets
*Lack of romance
*In-laws
*Interaction with Ex's
*Sharing home responsibilities
*Making decisions without discussing it first

Trouble Communicating? Here are some great conversation starters for a weekly date night.

Date Night Communication Questions

1. What was a win for you this week at work?

2. What was a win for you this week personally?

3. What was a win for us as a couple?

4. Did I miss an opportunity to give you credit for an accomplishment?

5. How can I better support you and your dreams?

6. What did I do this week that showed you I love you and care about you?

7. What could I have done that showed you I love you and care about you?

8. Are we as a couple moving toward our stated purpose and our shared vision?

9. Do you have any regrets from this week?

10. What can we do to make next week better than this week?

Simplified

Remember, if you don't learn to communicate with your spouse, your marriage will never reach its full potential or worse, it will completely fail.

Words are so incredibly powerful. That's why it's so important that we be intentional about speaking positive words to our spouse. Our words have the power to give life or death. Words can build up or tear down. Words unite or divide. Words can heal or hurt. Words can bring peace or war. Choose to speak encouragement, speak hope, speak joy, and speak love.

Challenge: The challenge is to sit down with your spouse and discuss the strengths and weaknesses of each other's personalities. Commit to each other to help the other stay away from the weaknesses and live in the strengths.

Say this to each other today. (You fill in the blanks.) "I know I don't say this enough, but I really want you to know that I _____ you, and you have made me a better _____ . I am extremely grateful for _____. I really truly mean it."

Prayer this today: *Lord, thank you for who you have made me to be. I accept myself, just the way you made me. I refuse to live in the weakness of my personality. But I will strive to live in my strengths. Give me the grace to walk this out and to live this out each day that I live.* **In Jesus' name, Amen.**

Discussion Questions

Rate yourself on a scale of 1-5, on whether or not you are communicating effectively. (1 is poor, 5 is excellent) Share it.

1........................2........................3........................4........................5

1. When do you and your spouse communicate the best?

_____
_____
_____
_____
_____
_____

2. What seems to be the most difficult time to communicate?

_____
_____
_____
_____
_____
_____

3. What are some of your greatest challenges when it comes to communicating?

_____
_____
_____
_____
_____

4. Have you identified your personality type?   If so what is it? Describe how you see it in your marriage and life.

_____
_____
_____
_____
_____
_____

5. Have you identified your spouse's personality type? If so, what is it? Describe how you see it.

_____
_____
_____
_____
_____
_____

6. Can you name an example of how you operate in your weaknesses?

_____
_____
_____
_____
_____
_____

7. Can you name an example of how you operate in your strength(s)?

_____
_____
_____
_____
_____
_____

8. How do you resolve disagreements?

_____
_____
_____
_____
_____

9. Do you feel like it is useless to try to resolve a disagreement? Why?

_____
_____
_____
_____
_____
_____

10. What is the best way to resolve a disagreement?

_____

_____

_____

_____

_____

_____

11. Do you feel like you need help/counseling to learn to communicate better? Why?

_____

_____

_____

_____

_____

_____

12. In what ways are you willing to get help? Write your commitment.

_____

_____

_____

_____

_____

_____

13. What steps can you take to better communicate with your spouse?

_____

_____

_____

_____

_____

Personal Strengths and Weaknesses Chart

POPULAR SANGUINE

"THE TALKER"

Motivated by: Fun

Place on the team: Creative Person

Emotional Needs: Attention. Affection. Approval. Acceptance.

Strengths: Optimism. Enthusiastic. Motivational. Social.

Weaknesses: Unrealistic. Disorganized. Manipulative. Too Bubbly.

Very Open & Loud

Listens for what they can say!

POWERFUL CHOLERIC

"THE DOER"

Motivated by: Control

Place on the team: Leadership Person

Emotional Needs: Loyalty. Appreciation. Sense of Control. Credit for Work.

Strengths: Results Oriented. Bottom Line. Direct. Decisive.

Weaknesses: Aggressive. Impatient. Domineering. Insensitive.

Very Strong & Commanding

Listens for the Bottom Line!

PEACEFUL PHLEGMATIC

"THE WATCHER"

Motivated by: Peace

Place on the team: Support Person

Emotional Needs: Peace & Quiet. Lack of Stress. Feeling of Worth. Respect.

Strengths: Harmonious. Helpful. Listener. Consistent.

Weaknesses: Passive. Insecure. Wishy-Washy. Non-Risky

Very Relaxed & Even-Paced

Listens by Picking Up on Emotion!

PERFECT MELANCHOLY

"THE THINKER"

Motivated by: Perfection

Place on the team: Detail Person

Emotional Needs: Sensitivity. Space. Support. Silence.

Strengths: Detailed Oriented. Logical. Systematic. Questioning.

Weaknesses: Critical. Hard to Please. Indecisive. Detached.

Very Closed & Reserved.

Listens for the Details and Asks Questions!

Use the notes section to write notes, thoughts, ideas or questions.

Notes:_____

_____

_____

_____

_____

_____

_____

_____

_____

_____

_____

_____

_____

_____

_____

_____

_____

_____

_____

_____

Use the notes section to write notes, thoughts, ideas or questions.

Notes:_____

_____

_____

_____

_____

_____

_____

_____

_____

_____

_____

_____

_____

_____

_____

_____

_____

_____

_____

_____

_____

_____

Use the notes section to write notes, thoughts, ideas or questions.

Notes:_____

_____

_____

_____

_____

_____

_____

_____

_____

_____

_____

_____

_____

_____

_____

_____

_____

_____

_____

_____

_____

_____

_____

Use the notes section to write notes, thoughts, ideas or questions.

Notes:_____

_____

_____

_____

_____

_____

_____

_____

_____

_____

_____

_____

_____

_____

_____

_____

_____

_____

_____

_____

_____

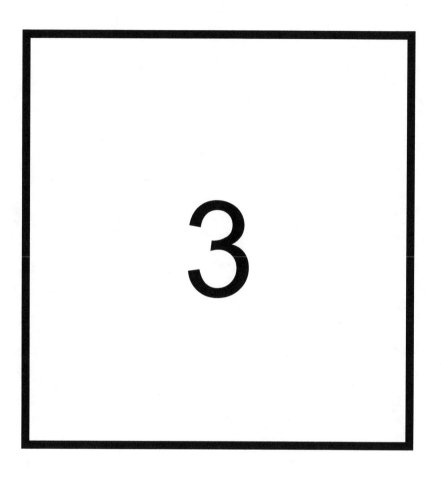

Chapter Three

_____

"Did God really say, 'You must not eat from any tree in the garden?'"

—**Genesis 3:1**

"Satan's very first attack against God's first marriage was an attack on the only boundary God had given them. Be assured, he will attack your boundaries as well."

—Kendall Bridges

"I have posted watchmen on your walls; pray to the Lord day and night for the fulfillment of his promises. Take no rest all you who pray."

—**Isaiah 62:6** (NLT)

"To be careful, stay alert, be aware be watchful! Watch out for attacks from the devil, your great enemy. He prowls around like a roaring lion, looking for some victim to devour."

—**1 Peter 5:8** (NLT paraphrased)

"Take a firm stand against him (Satan) and be strong in your faith."

—**1 Peter 5:9 (NLT Paraphrased)**

Here are some practical areas in our lives where we need to set boundaries.

1.   GUARD YOUR _____.

When you enter your house say _"peace be to this house"_ as it says

—**Luke 10:5** (Paraphrased).

"My people will live in safety, quietly at home. They will be at rest."

—**Isaiah 32:18** (Life Application Bible)

2. GUARD YOUR _____.

"Fx your thoughts on what is true and honorable and right. Think about things that are pure and lovely and admirable. Think about things that are excellent and worthy of praise."
—**Philippians 4:8** (New Living Paraphrased)

"But I say, anyone who even looks at a woman (man) with lust in his (her) eyes has already committed adultery with her (him) in his (her) heart."
—**Matthew 5:28** (NLT paraphrased)

3. GUARD YOUR _____.

Above all else, guard your heart, for it affects everything you do.
—**Proverbs 4:23** (NLT)

Another version says, "it determines the course of your life."

"His peace will guard your hearts as you live in Christ Jesus."
—**Philippians 4:7** (NLT Paraphrased)

"Love the Lord with all your heart, all your soul, and all your strength."
—**Deuteronomy 6:5** (NLT)

"The LORD is close to the brokenhearted; He rescues those whose spirits are crushed."
—**Psalm 34:18** (NLT)

"The Spirit of the LORD is upon Me,... He has sent Me to heal the brokenhearted..."
—**Luke 4:18** (NKJV)

4. GUARD YOUR _____.

"Set a guard over my mouth, keep watch over the door of my lips."
—**Psalms 141:3** (ESV)

Let everything you say be good and helpful, so that your words will be an encouragement to all those who hear them.
—**Ephesians 4:29** (NLT Paraphrased)

Gentle words bring life and health; a deceitful tongue crushes the spirit.
—**Proverbs 15:4** (NLT)

"Those who love to talk will experience the consequences, for the tongue can kill or nourish life."

—**Proverbs 18:21** (NLT)

5. GUARD YOUR _____.

A. First, your body belongs to God.

"Don't you know that your body is the temple of the Holy Spirit, who lives in you and was given to by God? You do not belong to yourself. For God bought you with a high price. So, you must honor God with your body."

—**I Corinthians 6: 19-20** (NLT Paraphrased)

B. Second, your body belongs to your spouse.

"The wife gives authority over her body to her husband, and the husband also gives authority over his body to his wife."

—**1 Corinthians 7:4**

C. Third, our body does not belong to anyone else—period!

"Run away from sexual sin! No other sin so clearly affects the body as this one does. For sexual immorality is a sin against your own body.

I Corinthians 6:18

6. GUARD YOUR _____.

"*Look straight ahead, and fix your eyes on what lies before you. Mark out a straight path for your feet, then stick to the path and stay safe. Don't get sidetracked; keep your feet from following evil.*"

—**Proverbs 4:25-27** (NLT)

7. GUARD YOUR _____.

- With God.
- With your spouse.
- With your children.

Simplified

Remember, boundaries are beneficial in all areas of life. Without boundaries, there would be total chaos. When you set up boundaries, you are setting up roadblocks to keep yourself out of harm's way. **You're not only drawing a line that you won't cross; you're drawing a line that you won't let the enemy cross.**

Challenge: Discuss with your spouse the boundaries that make you feel safer in your relationship. Then discuss the areas where you feel most vulnerable. Where do you need boundaries?

Pray this today: *Lord, help us establish healthy boundaries that will protect our marriage from all outside attacks. Help us to see the areas where we are most vulnerable. Help us to be honest enough to recognize the weak areas. Thank you for guarding our marriage and making it healthy and strong.* ***In Jesus' name, Amen.***

Discussion Questions

Rate yourself on a scale of 1-5, on whether or not you have effective boundaries for your marriage. (1 is poor, 5 is excellent) Share it.

1..................................2..................................3..................................4..........................5

1. **Guard Your Home**

   - Do you consider your home a safe place or a place of peace? Why or why not?

   _____
   _____
   _____
   _____
   _____
   _____
   _____
   _____

   - What are the main areas that Satan tries to attack your home?

   _____
   _____
   _____
   _____
   _____
   _____
   _____
   _____

   - What steps can you take to guard your home?

   _____
   _____
   _____
   _____
   _____
   _____
   _____
   _____

2. **Guard Your Mind**

   - How has the media created false ideas of marriage or relationships?

_____
_____
_____
_____
_____
_____
_____
_____

- Has your choice of entertainment had a positive or negative effect on your marriage?

_____
_____
_____
_____
_____
_____
_____
_____

- What steps can you take to guard your mind?

_____
_____
_____
_____
_____
_____
_____
_____

3. **Guard Your Heart**

- Why is your heart so important?

_____
_____
_____
_____
_____
_____

- How has God healed your heart in the past?

_____
_____
_____
_____
_____
_____

- What steps can you take to guard your heart?

_____
_____
_____
_____
_____
_____
_____

4. **Guard Your Mouth**

- What are words that hurt you?

_____
_____
_____
_____
_____
_____
_____

- What are words that build you up?

_____
_____
_____
_____
_____
_____
_____

- What steps can you take to guard your mouth?

_____
_____
_____
_____
_____
_____
_____

5. **Guard Your Body**

- If our body belongs to God first, how can we honor God with our body?

_____
_____
_____
_____
_____
_____
_____

- If our body belongs to our spouse second, how can we honor our spouse with our body?

_____
_____
_____
_____
_____
_____
_____

- What steps can you take to guard your body?

_____
_____
_____
_____
_____
_____
_____

6. **Guard Your Path**

- Have you set agreed upon boundaries for your marriage? If yes, name a few. If no, what are some boundaries you would like to see established?

_____
_____
_____
_____
_____
_____

- What steps can you take to guard your path?

_____
_____
_____
_____
_____
_____

7. **Guard Your Time**

- How can you guard your time with God?

_____
_____
_____
_____
_____
_____
_____

- How can you guard your time with your spouse?

_____
_____
_____
_____
_____
_____
_____

- How can you guard your time with your children?

_____
_____
_____
_____
_____
_____
_____

Use the notes section to write notes, thoughts, ideas or questions.

Notes:_____

_____

_____

_____

_____

_____

_____

_____

_____

_____

_____

_____

_____

_____

_____

_____

_____

_____

_____

_____

_____

Use the notes section to write notes, thoughts, ideas or questions.

Notes:_____

_____

_____

_____

_____

_____

_____

_____

_____

_____

_____

_____

_____

_____

_____

_____

_____

_____

_____

_____

Use the notes section to write notes, thoughts, ideas or questions.

Notes:_____

_____

_____

_____

_____

_____

_____

_____

_____

_____

_____

_____

_____

_____

_____

_____

_____

_____

_____

_____

Use the notes section to write notes, thoughts, ideas or questions.

Notes:_____

_____

_____

_____

_____

_____

_____

_____

_____

_____

_____

_____

_____

_____

_____

_____

_____

_____

_____

_____

_____

_____

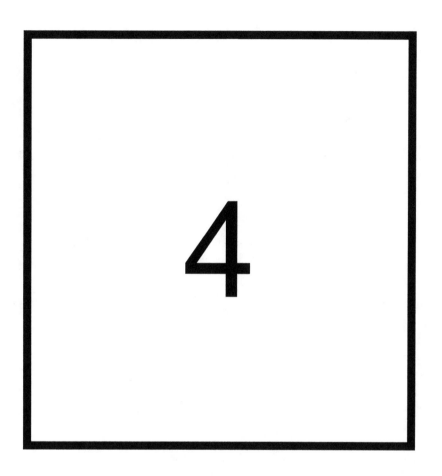

Chapter Four

"Dear children, let's not merely say that we love each other; let us show the truth by our actions."

—1 John 3:18 (NLT)

The greatest gift that you can give to others is the gift of unconditional love and acceptance.

—Brian Tracy

The Love Chapter— 1 Corinthians 13

Here's how to Love Right—God's Way.

Check out this paraphrased version of 1 Corinthians 13:4-8

"Love is patient. It is willing to wait. Love helps others, without wanting credit. Love doesn't look for greener pastures. Love doesn't brag or boast or build itself up to be something it isn't. Love doesn't take advantage of others. Love doesn't seek to take, but it generously gives. Love doesn't get mad, blow up and turn on and off. Love doesn't think about how it could get back at someone. Love grieves over the evil and pain in this world. Love rejoices when truth wins. Love comes and sits with you when you're feeling down and finds out what is wrong. Love empathizes with you and believes in you. Love stands by your side and cheers you on when you fall. Love doesn't give up, quit, or walk out in tough times. Love keeps going strong when everything goes wrong. Love wins, because God wins. That, my friend, is what real love is!"

I would like you to take these one portion at a time and rate yourself on how you are measuring up to God's definition of love.

Remember...Never settle for good enough. It can always be better.

No one will be perfect. Believe me, we're not after perfection. No one is perfect but Jesus. But if we can identify areas where we are weak, then we can work on getting better in those areas.

Love Evaluation

Let's look at these definitions of love from the Bible and rate yourself on a scale of 1-5.

(1 is poor and 5 is excellent). As you read each statement, replace the word "love" with your own name. For example, "Kendall/Starla is patient. Kendall/Starla is willing to wait."

- *Love is patient. It is willing to wait.*

  1................................2................................3................................4................................5

- *Love helps others, without wanting credit.*

  1................................2................................3................................4................................5

- *Love doesn't look for greener pastures.*

  1................................2................................3................................4................................5

- *Love doesn't brag or boast or build itself up to be something it isn't.*

  1................................2................................3................................4................................5

- *Love doesn't take advantage of others.*

  1................................2................................3................................4................................5

- *Love doesn't seek to take, but it generously gives.*

  1................................2................................3................................4................................5

- *Love doesn't get mad, blow up and turn on and off.*

  1................................2................................3................................4................................5

- *Love doesn't think about how it could get back at someone.*

  1................................2................................3................................4................................5

- *Love grieves over the evil and pain in this world.*

  1................................2................................3................................4................................5

- *Love rejoices when truth wins.*

  1................................2................................3................................4................................5

- *Love comes and sits with you when you're feeling down and finds out what is wrong.*

I................2................3................4................5

- *Love empathizes with you and believes in you.*

I................2................3................4................5

- *Love stands by your side and cheers you on when you fall.*

I................2................3................4................5

- *Love doesn't give up, quit, or walk out in tough times.*

I................2................3................4................5

- *Love keeps going strong when everything goes wrong.*

I................2................3................4................5

- *Love Wins, because God wins. That, my friend, is what real love is!*

That is a true definition of love. It is the exact opposite of what our culture says love is. Sincere love requires concentration and effort. It means helping others become better people.

> Don't just pretend to love others. Really love them. Hate what is wrong. Hold tightly to what is good. Love each other with genuine affection, and take delight in honoring each other.
>
> **—Romans 12:9-10 (NLT)**

You see, there is a big difference between the love that we experience when we are dating (emotional love) that consumes us and literally blinds us to the realities of whom we are dating, and the love that sustains a marriage for years to come—(the attitude of love.)

One is *emotional*. The other is an *attitude*.

One *drives* you. The other you must *drive*.

One *commands* you. The other you must *command*.

The beautiful thing is that once the emotional love wears off and you get down to "real life," you can operate in the right "attitude of love" and the "emotions" will follow.

Is it possible to stay in love for a lifetime? Absolutely. You just have to make the right choice.

The emotional love or "honeymoon love" as some call it, will tend to fade, but that's when you have to make a choice and choose the attitude of love. Love is a choice that you have to make when emotions fade away.

.Love Languages

When you love the right way, God's way, an amazing world of fulfillment opens up before you.

Gary Chapman's *Five Love Languages* (5lovelanguages.com)

1. Words of Affirmation
2. Acts of Service
3. Receiving Gifts
4. Quality Time
5. Physical Touch

LOVING TRANSPARENT

God intended the love between a husband and wife to be completely transparent.

A. If you are ashamed of your sin—Know that **1 John 1:9** (ESV) says, "If we confess our sins, he is faithful and just to forgive us our sins and to cleanse us from all unrighteousness."

B. If you live in fear of not being loved—Read **1 John 4:18** (NLT Paraphrased), "Such love has no fear because perfect love expels all fear."

Every secret is a layer, every layer causes division between you and your spouse.

Wherever secrecy lives, intimacy dies. You have to let go of the past.

Simplified

Loving right—God's Way, is loving unconditionally – because of what your love can do for them, not what they can do for you. Then, you must learn the language of love so your love can be heard and experienced. Lastly, you must choose to live and love transparent. Remember, where secrecy lives, intimacy dies.

Challenge: Take the love language test at 5lovelanguages.com so that you can understand what your love language is and most importantly, so you will know what your spouse's love language is. Then, be intentional each day this week to do something specifically that communicates your love in their language.

Pray this today: *Lord, help us to love unconditionally, the way you loved us. Teach us how to love in a way that does not expect anything in return. Let us find the joy in loving your way. Help us to be more transparent with our fears and concerns and help us to be able to respond to my one and only with the love and support they need. **In Jesus' name, Amen**.*

Discussion Questions

Rate yourself on a scale of 1-5, on whether or not you are Loving Right—God's Way.
(1 is poor, 5 is excellent) Share it.

1.........................2.........................3.........................4.........................5

1. According to **1 Corinthians 13:4-8,** list five things that love is.

    _____

    _____

    _____

    _____

    _____

    _____

    _____

2. How does the definition of love in 1 Corinthians 13 differ from our culture today?

    _____

    _____

    _____

    _____

    _____

    _____

3. What is the difference between "emotional" love and the "attitude" of love?

    _____

    _____

    _____

    _____

    _____

    _____

4. Can you identify your love language?

    _____

    _____

    _____

    _____

    _____

5. Can you identify your spouse's love language?

_____
_____
_____
_____
_____
_____
_____

6. What is something you could do this week to communicate your love in his/her language?

_____
_____
_____
_____
_____
_____
_____

7. What is something your spouse could do to communicate their love to you this week?

_____
_____
_____
_____
_____
_____
_____

8. What are some of the next steps you can take for you to love the right way—God's way?

_____
_____
_____
_____
_____
_____

Use the notes section to write notes, thoughts, ideas or questions.

Notes:_____

_____

_____

_____

_____

_____

_____

_____

_____

_____

_____

_____

_____

_____

_____

_____

_____

_____

_____

_____

Use the notes section to write notes, thoughts, ideas or questions.

Notes:_____

_____

_____

_____

_____

_____

_____

_____

_____

_____

_____

_____

_____

_____

_____

_____

_____

_____

_____

_____

_____

_____

Use the notes section to write notes, thoughts, ideas or questions.

Notes:_____

_____

_____

_____

_____

_____

_____

_____

_____

_____

_____

_____

_____

_____

_____

_____

_____

_____

_____

_____

Use the notes section to write notes, thoughts, ideas or questions.

Notes:_____

_____

_____

_____

_____

_____

_____

_____

_____

_____

_____

_____

_____

_____

_____

_____

_____

_____

_____

_____

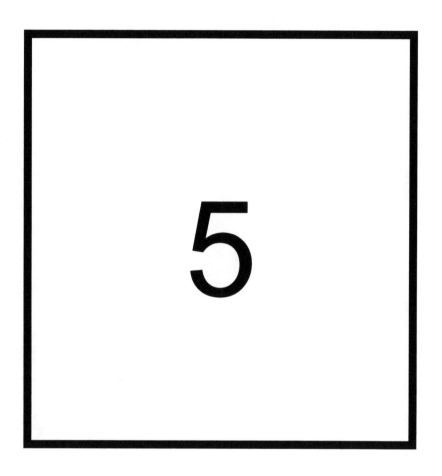

Chapter Five

Dying to self

"Father, if you are willing, take this cup from me; yet not my will, but yours be done."

—**Luke 22:42** (NIV)

"Almost every sinful action ever committed can be traced back to a selfish motive. It is a trait we hate in other people but justify in ourselves."

—Stephen Kendrick, <u>The Love Dare</u>

Gethsemane is a garden at the foot of the Mount of Olives in <u>Jerusalem</u>. It is most famous for being the place where Jesus prayed and his disciples slept the night before <u>his arrest and crucifixion</u>. Jesus often prayed in this garden, which allowed Judas to find him on the night of His betrayal and arrest.

The name *"Gethsemane"* comes from an Aramaic word, meaning "*oil press.*" Oil is pressed, squeezed and ground out of the olives in order to preserve the oil and use it for its intended purposes.

This is where Jesus chose to wrestle with His flesh. This is where His will was pressed, squeezed and relinquished.

This is where Jesus sweat, drops of blood, as he agonized over submitting to the will of His Father, rather than an easier path. This is where He surrendered His will to the Father, once and for all, to be the sacrifice for our sins.

What does all of this have to do with our marriages? Selfishness. We must die to selfishness.

The Bible tells us in **John 12:24:** *"Very truly I tell you, unless a kernel of wheat falls to the ground and dies, it remains only a single seed. But if it dies, it produces many seeds."*

This means that in order for some things to live, other things must die. In order for the *better marriage* that is in each of you to live, each husband and wife must be willing to die to their own agenda, so that a shared agenda can live.

Die to Your Self

This is what happens to us when we put our lives in the hands of Christ and allow Him to bury the old man, the old nature and the flesh that continues to try to find its way in our lives. The old man is buried and the new man is born.

"If any person be in Christ, he is a new creature, the old is gone and the new has come."

—**2 Corinthians 5:17**

Thank God for new life. We may not be what we want to be. But thank God, we're not what we used to be.
Those who belong to Christ Jesus have crucified the flesh with its passions and desires.

—**Galatians 5:24**

If we are going to be fully devoted followers of Christ, we must die to ourselves and crucify the flesh, each and every day.

And whoever does not carry their cross and follow me cannot be my disciple.

—**Luke 14:27**

But every one of us have found that this is not a one-time battle. The flesh continues to try to find its way in our lives each day, which is why the Apostle Paul says in **1 Corinthians 15:31,** *"I die daily."*

The entire process of dying to self is moving from a *"me first"* way of living to a *"you first"* way of living.

If you will humble yourself and die to yourself on behalf of your marriage, God will raise you up to places, positions and favor that you could never imagine. In this place of sacrifice and surrender is where you will find real fulfillment in marriage.

Notice in the scripture below how Christ chose to humble Himself for us, through death. And because of His surrender, God raised Him up to a place of authority to be the salvation for all mankind.

Philippians 2:1-9 (MSG)

2 ¹⁻⁴ If you've gotten anything at all out of following Christ, if his love has made any difference in your life, if being in a community of the Spirit means anything to you, if you have a heart, if you care—then do me a favor: Agree with each other, love each other, be deep-spirited friends. Don't push your way to the front; don't sweet-talk your way to the top. Put yourself aside, and help others get ahead. Don't be obsessed with getting your own advantage. Forget yourselves long enough to lend a helping hand.

⁵⁻⁸ Think of yourselves the way Christ Jesus thought of himself. He had equal status with God but didn't think so much of himself that he had to cling to the advantages of that status no matter what. Not at all. When the time came, he set aside the privileges of deity and took on the status of a slave, became human! Having become human, he stayed human. It was an incredibly humbling process. He didn't claim special privileges. Instead, he lived a selfless, obedient life and then died a selfless, obedient death—and the worst kind of death at that—a crucifixion.

⁹⁻¹¹ Because of that obedience, God lifted him high and honored him far beyond anyone or anything, ever, so that all created beings in heaven and on earth—even those long ago dead and buried—will bow in worship before this Jesus Christ, and call out in praise that he is the Master of all, to the glorious honor of God the Father.

Dying to yourself is hard. Even Jesus prayed to God that if there was any other way, He was open to it. But at the end of the day, Jesus said, "Not my will, but yours be done." It was not His will that ruled, it was the will of His Heavenly Father. This is exactly the way we need to live our lives and function in our marriage. At the end of the day, it's not our will, plans or desires that matter. It is only the will of God that matters. Surrender to His will, die to your flesh. Die to your plans and your desires and watch great things begin to happen for you, as God's plans begin to come alive in you and your marriage.

Simplified

Dying to yourself is hard. Even Jesus prayed to God, that if there was any other way, He was open to it. But at the end of the day, Jesus said, not my will, but yours be done. It was not His will that ruled, it was the will of His Heavenly Father. This is exactly the way we need to live our lives and function in our marriage. At the end of the day, it's not our will, plans or desires that matter. It is only the will of God that matters. Surrender to His will, die to your flesh. Die to your plans and your desires and watch great things begin to happen for you, as God's plans begin to come alive in you and your marriage.

Challenge: Sit down together with your spouse and talk about the dreams that you have. What dreams are pulling you apart and what dreams are drawing you closer together? This will be difficult, but there may have to be some compromise and negotiation regarding what dreams and plans you choose as a couple to embrace and move forward with. Don't allow selfishness to enter into this discussion. Don't try to hold someone hostage to give up something that they really desire. Pray about it and find a workable solution that works for you both. Remember in the end, both must win.

Pray this today: *Lord, we choose today to die to our will and our individual dreams, so that a unified dream can live within us. We commit to put you first, each other second and ourselves last. We believe that you have an incredible dream for our marriage. We believe it is better than we have ever imagined. We ask that you help us walk it out and live it out, each day.* **In Jesus' name, Amen.**

Discussion Questions

Rate yourself on a scale of 1-5, on whether or not you are daily dying to yourself. (1 is poor, 5 is excellent)

Share it.

1................................2................................3................................4........................5

1. The word Gethsemane means "oil press." In the garden of Gethsemane Jesus prayed, "Not my will but yours be done." His will was pressed and squeezed out of Him. What does this have to do with marriage?

    _____
    _____
    _____
    _____
    _____
    _____

2. Do you struggle with your will or wanting your way in marriage? Or have you discovered a way to find common ground when you have opposing opinions? Explain your answer.

    _____
    _____
    _____
    _____
    _____
    _____

3. Where does your flesh or will give you the biggest problems?

    _____
    _____
    _____
    _____
    _____
    _____

4. Are you afraid or reluctant to let go of your dreams and trust God for a shared dream to be realized? If so, why?

_____
_____
_____
_____
_____
_____

5. What are some of your best shared spiritual experiences together as a couple?

_____
_____
_____
_____
_____
_____

6. What are some of your dreams and goals together as a couple?

_____
_____
_____
_____
_____
_____

7. What steps can you take to die to yourself?

_____
_____
_____
_____
_____
_____

Notes:

_____
_____
_____
_____
_____
_____

Use the notes section to write notes, thoughts, ideas or questions.

Notes:_____

_____

_____

_____

_____

_____

_____

_____

_____

_____

_____

_____

_____

_____

_____

_____

_____

_____

_____

_____

Use the notes section to write notes, thoughts, ideas or questions.

Notes:_____

_____

_____

_____

_____

_____

_____

_____

_____

_____

_____

_____

_____

_____

_____

_____

_____

_____

_____

_____

_____

_____

_____

Use the notes section to write notes, thoughts, ideas or questions.

Notes:_____

_____

_____

_____

_____

_____

_____

_____

_____

_____

_____

_____

_____

_____

_____

_____

_____

_____

_____

Use the notes section to write notes, thoughts, ideas or questions.

Notes:_____

_____

_____

_____

_____

_____

_____

_____

_____

_____

_____

_____

_____

_____

_____

_____

_____

_____

_____

_____

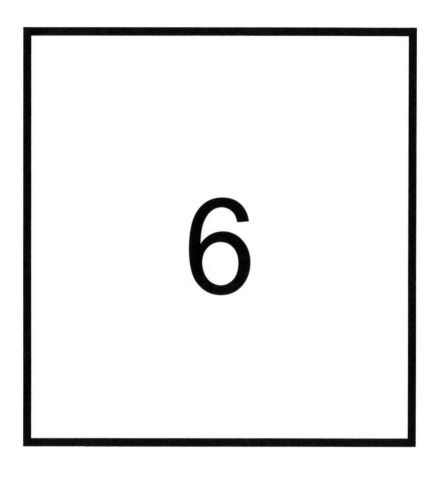

Bonus Chapter

Sex

Sexual intimacy in marriage is incredible; it's to be protected and cherished.   It's the act of becoming one flesh, connecting emotionally, physically and spiritually. It's more than just a few moments of pleasure. It is knowing, and being fully known, loving without any walls. It is seeing all—knowing all and loving all. It is trusting each other with the most intimate and delicate parts of our body. It is serving and pleasing one another. It is a bond that strengthens a marriage.

A. What does the Bible say about sex and marriage?

- **Sex is for marriage and marriage is for sex.**

  "Therefore a man shall leave his father and his mother and hold fast to his wife, and they shall become one flesh."

  —**Genesis 1:24**

  "One flesh" refers to sexual and spiritual unity between a man and a woman.

  God designed sex to be so intense, fulfilling and memorable that He wants us to share it with our "One and Only" for a lifetime.

  God is definitely not opposed to sex! We're all happy about that. Can I get an Amen?

- **Is sex before marriage wrong? Yes.**

  In **Mark 7:20** Jesus lists a number of sins. Two of them are "sexual immorality" and "adultery." Sexual immorality refers to sex before marriage. Adultery refers to having sex with someone who is not your spouse, while you are married.

"But, since sexual immorality is occurring, each man should have sexual relations with his own wife, and each woman with her own husband."

—1 Corinthians 7:2

The way to avoid sexual immorality is to have "your own" husband or wife.

Here are some other verses that support this truth.

Hebrews 13:4; 1 Thessalonians 4:3-4; 1 Thessalonians 4:7; 1 Corinthians 6:18-20; Colossians 3:5

And also, in **Song of Solomon 2:7; 3:5; 8:4** it says, "Do not arouse or awaken love until it so desires."

In other words, save sex for marriage.

- **Is adultery a sin? Yes.**

C'mon man!!! It's one of the Big 10 Commandments!!!

"You shall not commit adultery."

—**Exodus 20:14**

You can't get around that. Unless you try to say, "But that is Old Testament." Well then, read what the New Testament says...

"What comes out of a person is what defiles them. For it is from within, out of a person's heart, that evil thoughts come—sexual immorality, theft, murder, **adultery,** greed, malice, deceit, lewdness, envy, slander, arrogance and folly. All these evils come from inside and defile a person."

—**Mark 7:20-22**

God's plan is and has always been to find complete fulfillment in your "One and Only."

May your fountain be blessed and may you rejoice in the wife of your youth.

—**Proverbs 5:18 (NIV)**

- **Is sex about having children or having fun? Both.**

"But a married man is concerned with...how he can please his wife...A married woman is concerned about ...how she can please her husband."

—**1 Corinthians 7:33-34**

Notice that we are to "please" or bring pleasure to our spouse.

May your fountain be blessed, and may you rejoice in the wife of your youth. A loving doe, a graceful deer—may her breasts satisfy you always, may you ever be intoxicated with her love.

—Proverbs 5:18-19 (NIV)

We are to enjoy the sexual experience with our spouse so much that it leaves us as if we were intoxicated and cannot walk straight. Now that's what I'm talking about!

- **How often should a married couple have sex? Depends.**

Do not deprive each other except perhaps by **mutual consent** and for a time, so that you may devote yourselves to prayer. Then come together again so that Satan will not tempt you because of your lack of self-control.

—1 Corinthians 7:5

The key in this verse is "mutual consent." Really this is the key to all of your marriage decisions, whether they are sex related or not. You have to agree on what works best for you both. One spouse may want to have sex every day, while the other only wants to have sex once a month. What is the solution? Mutual consent. Agree to find a solution that you both agree on.

- **Is viewing pornography a sin? Yes.**

Matthew 5:28 is very clear: "But I tell you that anyone who looks at a woman lustfully has already committed adultery with her in his heart."

If you view pornography alone or together as a couple, it is sin. **1 John 2:16** says, "For everything in the world—the cravings of sinful man, the **lust of his eyes** and the boasting of what he has and does—comes not from the Father but from the world."

Viewing porn just to get excited enough to have sex with each other is robbing each of you of the ultimate fulfillment in your marriage.

- **Is oral sex before marriage a sin? Yes.**

  Some dating couples opt for oral sex instead of intercourse, thinking that they are still saving themselves in some way.

  Look at what the scriptures say....

  But among you there must not be even a hint of sexual immorality, or of any kind of impurity, or of greed, because these are improper for God's holy people.
  —**Ephesians 5:3 (NIV)**

  Notice that the scriptures say that we should avoid even the hint of sexual immorality and any kind of impurity. This would include oral sex.

- **Is oral sex in a marriage relationship sin? It depends.**

  It is clear in scripture that the Song of Solomon refers to what could be defined as oral sex.

  Like an apple tree among the trees of the forest is my beloved among the young men. **I delight to sit in his shade, and his fruit is sweet to my taste.**
  —**Song of Solomon 2:3**

  Awake, north wind, and come, south wind! **Blow on my garden**, that its fragrance may spread everywhere. **Let my beloved come into his garden and taste its choice fruits.**
  —**Song of Solomon 4:16**

  But let me take you back to a foundational scripture for all of our marriages.

  "Marriage should be honored by all, and the marriage bed kept pure (undefiled), for God will judge the adulterer and all the sexually immoral."
  —**Hebrews 13:4**

  One of the ways that you keep the marriage bed pure or "undefiled" is to always be in agreement with one another regarding what is acceptable and what is not in your sexual relationship. No spouse should ever feel forced or pressured to perform in any way that is uncomfortable to them. God created the sexual relationship to be enjoyed and celebrated between a husband and a wife. Period. Nothing else is condoned in scriptures.

- **Sex is not a dirty word!**

  It's very clear that God is pro-sex and has given us plenty of guidelines for what sex should look like in a marriage.

  Sex should not be hidden because it is dirty. It should be protected because it's precious. God has given us rules and boundaries to protect this sacred treasure that we share with our spouse.

- **What if I have blown it? Is there any hope for my marriage? Yes, yes and yes.**

  Let me say this, every marriage can be restored, if both husband and wife are willing to do whatever it takes to make it work. Our job is to repent and commit to following the ways of Jesus Christ. **(Psalm 51:7; 1 John 1:9)** It may take a long time to find healing, restoration and forgiveness. But we are living testimonies that God can take a marriage that appeared to be D.O.A. and breathe His life-giving power into it and cause it to live again. It will be an uphill climb, but if you will commit to change your heart and surrender to Christ, anything is possible. Then, with the help of a qualified counselor, good friends and a Great Big God, you can have the Better Marriage that you are dreaming of.

Let's talk about Foreplay.

Foreplay will most likely look different to you than it does to your spouse. A great start is flirting with each other, laughing together, playing together, de-stressing…Great sex starts with great foreplay, great foreplay starts with loving right.

Let's refer to Chapter Four, "Loving Right" where we talk about love languages. When you know what your spouse's love language is, you will know the best way to turn your spouse on.

For instance, if your spouse's love language is:

• **"Physical Touch"**—Get yourself some oils, turn on some music and start massaging, foot massage, back massage, hand massage, whatever makes them happy. If you don't know, ask.

• **"Acts of Service"**—Help your spouse around the house. See what needs to be done and do it. Wash the dishes, straighten the house, bathe the kids or help with the laundry. Or do something they've wanted you to do for a long time.

- **"Words of Affirmation"**—Talk to your spouse, tell them things you love about them, what you appreciate about them, what a great job they are doing, how proud of them you are and why.

- **"Gifts"**—Bring home your spouse's favorite candy, drink or surprise them with something they've been wanting (jewelry/shoes/golf club).

- **"Quality Time"**—Spend time with them, put down the phone, make obvious efforts to be with them doing things they love to do (walking, shopping, a movie, a game, a getaway, hiking, a vacation they've been talking about).

If you don't care enough to learn your spouse's love language and sexual needs, you are selfish, and selfish sex is unsatisfying.

Common causes for low or no sex drive:

Hormonal imbalances, physical pain, your body not functioning the way it should.

Sickness or disease.

Depression, anxiety, low self-esteem, lack of confidence.

Addiction to alcohol, illegal or over the counter drugs.

Exhaustion, feeling stressed or overwhelmed.

Emotional pain from being sexually abused.

Adultery, porn addiction and unforgiveness will kill intimacy with your spouse.

Don't let any of these issues be ignored; they won't just go away on their own. Talk to your spouse. Pray together, ask God to heal you and direct you to the help that is needed.

(Jimmy Evans does a great teaching on "Creating Sexual Intimacy." Check it out at MarriageToday.com)

Satan knows how damaging sex outside of God's plan can be. That's why he has used sex as his main weapon to destroy so many lives.

He also knows how powerful a healthy life sex between a husband and wife can be.

Sex outside of your marriage will destroy you.

Sex within your marriage will strengthen you.

Closing Statement

We know that marriage can be hard. It takes a lot of work to have a better marriage. But every effort you put into it will be worth it.

Keep investing in, working on, and praying for God's very best for you and your spouse. Your greatest days are ahead. The best is yet to come. We're praying for you and believing with you for all that God has prepared for you. Remember what the scripture says, *"Eye has not seen, ear has not heard, no mind has conceived what God has prepared for those who love Him."*

—1 Corinthians 2:9-10

Never settle for good enough—your marriage can always be better!

—Kendall and Starla Bridges

Resources & Recommendations

Never stop investing in and improving your marriage.

Here are our recommendations for other resources that we have found helpful.

The Bible is and always will be the very best marriage manual ever written!

Jimmy and Karen Evans at Marriage Today— marriagetoday.com

Florence Littauer's "Personality Plus"— temperamentquiz.com

Gary Chapman's "5 Love Languages"—5lovelanguages.com

Dave Ramsey's Financial Peace University— daveramsey.com/fpu

Francis and Lisa Chan's "You and Me Forever"

Follow us on social media and let us hear from you.

Bettermarriage365.com

@bettermarriage365

#bettermarriage365

kendallbridges.com

About The Authors

Kendall and Starla Bridges met in Bible College in August 1981, married in August 1982, had their first of four children in August 1983. They have two sons and two daughters, all married, beautiful and world changers. They have nine grandchildren that are the best ever! So much fun! 3 boys and 6 girls, who call them "Pops and Shoobie." They pastor Freedom Church in Carrollton, Texas, where their mission is "helping people find freedom." If you're ever in the Dallas area they would love for you to visit.

Find out more about Freedom Church

findfreedom.church @findfreedom.church

Kendall and Starla authored their first book together *Better Marriage Against All Odds* telling their story of being married, broken, and then restored (available on Amazon). They also travel and speak at marriage conferences, date nights and weekend services to share their story as well as equip couples to have the beautiful, better marriage God intended for all of us to have.

You can follow their journey at betternmarriage365.com, @bettermarriage365 , or on Facebook Better Marriage 365!

Use the notes section to write notes, thoughts, ideas or questions.

Notes:_____

_____

_____

_____

_____

_____

_____

_____

_____

_____

_____

_____

_____

_____

_____

_____

_____

_____

_____

CPSIA information can be obtained
at www.ICGtesting.com
Printed in the USA
FFHW012201150719
53665602-59331FF